ACCLAIM FOR
Personal Happiness

"Being a woman in business has its own set of
challenges. Being a woman in a male-dominated
industry such as financial services adds even more
to the list. Searching for that ever-elusive work/
life balance makes this a perfect trifecta to address.
Wendy Campbell's *Personal Happiness* hits it out
of the park with her professional takeaways and
personal stories. As someone who came through
the same challenges with my own battle scars, I
related to Wendy page by page. Opportunities don't
always come gift-wrapped. Be open to those that are
presented to you. Wendy's book is one opportunity to
get your arms around."

—Judy Hoberman, President, Selling in a Skirt

Personal Happiness

Learn to Balance
Your Home and Career

Wendy Campbell

PASSIONQUEST
Technologies LLC

Personal Happiness
Learn to Balance Your Home and Career
Copyright © 2015 Wendy Campbell

PassionQuest Technologies
5055 Business Center Drive
Suite 108, PMB 110
Fairfield, CA 94534
Phone: 707-688-2848
Fax: 707-402-6319
Email: info@earnprofitsfromyourpassion.com

PASSIONQUEST
Technologies LLC

Cover and book design by Cypress House
Front cover image: © iStock.com/soleg

Publisher's Cataloging-in-Publication Data

Campbell, Wendy (Wendy C.), 1975-

  Personal happiness : learn to balance your home and career / Wendy Campbell. -- First edition. -- Fairfield, CA : PassionQuest Technologies LLC, [2015]

  pages ; cm.

  ISBN: 978-0-9912611-1-6

  Summary: Inspirational book for women about being career oriented and keeping a stable family life.--Publisher.

  1. Work-life balance. 2. Work and family. 3. Happiness. 4. Businesswomen. 5. Working mothers. 6. Women--Family relationships. 7. Job satisfaction. 8. Success in business. 9. Quality of life. 10. Quality of work life. 11. Self-actualization (Psychology) I. Title.

HD4904.25 .C36 2015   2015906376
650.1--dc23   1507

Printed in the USA
2 4 6 8 9 7 5 3 1
First edition

Dedication

I dedicate this book to my daughter, Tracee, my most precious and dear baby girl—"Sis" we call her, now an incredibly wonderful young woman. And to the friends who have helped me see better ways to be. To my mom and grandmothers, and their guidance, spoken and understood; to my sister whose example is beyond measure; and to my female cousins who have so many different views, giving me chances to look at life in different lights. I am so thankful. This book is dedicated to you all.

Permissions and Credits

Contents

Foreword

*T*wenty-five years ago I was a single mom with three small children, working four jobs and struggling to make ends meet. I didn't know who I was. I was too busy, too scared, and too tired to try to figure out anything but how to take care of my children.

Through the years, I became privileged to work with women in the financial services industry, and managed to create a successful career. In this business is where I met Wendy Campbell.

Reading Wendy's book, I thought how much I would have loved experiencing her life. She had such amazing grandmothers and mothers and friends who helped shape her. All the lessons she learned and the support she received from them were so important. They set a pace for Wendy as she became a wife, mother, friend, coworker, and influential leader of other women.

Wendy's book gave me the opportunity to reflect on all of the strong, compassionate women who have helped shape my own life. I realized then that for me, that legacy is the essence of this book and of Wendy Campbell.

This book's purpose is to reach out to its readers and have them remember and be grateful for all those generous women—mentors, teachers, bosses, family, and friends—who have positively impacted our lives. We can then better internalize and apply the lessons learned from these wonderful women.

Wendy's book truly succeeds beyond measure in its ability to deeply touch women of all ages. She has given readers a checklist of attributes every woman needs and a blueprint to share with other women in our lives. What a wonderful gift!

Anyone who can call Wendy friend, mom, neighbor, aunt, sister, daughter, granddaughter, coworker, boss, colleague, or author of your now favorite book... is blessed.

This book should be on every woman's nightstand as the go-to guide to reflect on who we are and what we can be.

Rebecca Rice
Manager and founder, Rebecca Rice & Associates, LLC

Introduction

*T*hroughout my life books have helped me in count-less ways. What I have learned from reading and absorbing information in good books has helped me become a better wife, given me stronger mothering skills, and made me a more effective human being as a daughter, granddaughter, aunt, sister and friend, among other things.

This book is for all women. It could serve as a coffee-table staple, or a friend on your nightstand, or an item on your kitchen shelf, to pick up lovingly as a guide and reference to solving trials and troubles that might fall into your path. Also, a wish from me to you is that in sharing some of the stories you will make a positive difference in the lives of those you love and care for.

I need you to know that serving others well is essential to a life well led.

Push, extend, stretch, and *give* of yourselves in your personal and professional lives. Show the good inside of you; use your gentleness, kindness, and compassion. Keep in the forefront peace, patience, love, and self-control.

To help you achieve the best results along your journey, I've placed strategic questions throughout this book. Each question is identified as a "Personal Happiness Challenge." I encourage you to interact with and reflect upon each question. Your time will be well spent.

Your proud legacy can be that others say your work was done right, done well, and done with goodness.

You can crash through that finish line healthy but exhausted—knowing you have been in the arena and fought, loved, and truly lived.

February 2015

Strong Women:
May we know them,
may we raise them,
may we be them.

Wendy Campbell

Chapter 1

Career Woman at Eighteen

I grew up in Norwood, Colorado, and had worked in a local insurance office there since my junior year in high school. I was quite the diligent hard worker. I knew just about everyone in the community and spent a lot of time helping people who had helped raise me (as in "It takes a village"). Even as a teenager, I realized the importance of taking care of the needs of community residents and that what I was doing mattered. That felt really good.

I give credit to my parents especially for teaching me to be a confident, responsible human being.

> *To accomplish great things one must*
> *not only act, but also dream.*
> *Not only plan, but also believe.*
> —Anatole France

Mom and Dad, not only did you dream of a great life you could create for your family, but you also made it happen. You always just made it happen. You worked tirelessly for us so that we could enjoy the fruits of your labor, and you did so happily. You taught me the true meaning of perseverance. I thank you for teaching us that life doesn't just hand you everything you want; that life deals you circumstances that are often unfair or unjust, and that's okay. Life isn't fair.

Dad, you taught me that with great determination and strength I can overcome almost all obstacles and if there are any that I can't overcome, your big strong arms will be there to catch my fall, and your constant coaching will lead me in the right direction. You never gave up on me on anything... ever.

Mom and Dad, you were always true believers and had so much conviction and strength in those beliefs. You believed that with hard work and dedication I could do anything I set my mind to. It all went so quickly to the time I was seventeen, leaving home, setting out on my own adventure to pursue my dreams. You never wavered. You never faltered. You never thought any of my dreams were foolish or impractical. You were the consummate optimists, the ultimate cheerleaders.

I thank you both so much for giving me all the necessary tools throughout my life to make me an independent, confident, successful woman. I thank you for always supporting my dreams and believing in me.

You are amazing parents and friends, and I am so very blessed to be your baby girl.

The harder I worked the more notice I received from my boss. Since he lived a few hours away at the time, his assessment of my work came from viewing company profit reports. The older women who worked in the office didn't appreciate my enthusiasm or my drive—I think the fact that I was so young intimidated them.

When I was a high school senior about to graduate, I was promoted to manager at the insurance agency, taking the place of a woman who had been there much longer than I. You can guess that didn't go over well.

I struggled daily with internal battles... Where did I belong? I would think *I'm only eighteen— do I even deserve this? Do I really know what I'm doing?* Such questions were in the forefront of my mind in those days. I realized then that it was very important to "not keep score" but to just do my job and do it well. If those in positions around or above me didn't like the situation, well, they weren't up for a challenge.

*Personal Happiness Challenge:
What internal battles do you face?*

I graduated from high school that May and married my high school sweetheart in July. We stayed in the area, and my new husband continued working on his family's ranch alongside his father. I was determined to continue my position with the agency. I decided to take on some decorating decisions at work—heck, I was the manager, why not? I redecorated the office, making dreary brown walls much more welcoming, and gave it a facelift that really blew my coworkers' minds— not in a good way, but in a "Who does she think she is?" way.

I can tell you who I was back in 1993: A determined, likable young lady who had made an impression by doing my job well. And when given the managerial position, responsibilities like making decisions about redecorating were part of it.

Personal Happiness Challenge:
Who are you? Who do you want to be?

Then, in November 1994, our son was born—the sweetest little thing you can imagine. Totally enthralled with the animals, he spent his days in his car seat, bundled up, hanging out on the ranch with his dad. Mom had to go into an office—yuck!

Our son, Brad, was four months old when my husband, Trace, and I finally had enough extra money to take our first real vacation. Grandma and Grandpa kept Brad, and Trace and I went to the Bahamas for the honeymoon we'd never had.

Lo and behold, our daughter, Tracee, was conceived on that trip; we like telling her that she was "made in the Bahamas." What were we thinking! We had a four-month-old baby at home.

In March 1996, our beautiful baby girl, whom we lovingly call Sis, graced us with her presence. And it dawned on us... now what? Trace can take Brad on workdays, but what am I going to do? Hey—I was the manager; I would take her with me. And I did. When you have the ability to call the shots in your career, you find out very quickly that you can do your job and have conveniences that you might not have working in a dead-end job... or not having the respect and authority that you could have. It's important to love what you do and have the surrounding support. If you don't, then work toward that. You'll be amazed at what you're able to free up in your day-to-day efforts.

Personal Happiness Challenge:
What do you love to do?

So I brought Tracee with me, not every day, but two days a week, and I kept this pattern for several months.

At that point baby Sis (Tracee) was way too busy to stay in a bouncy chair all day.

So between grandmas, grandpas, aunts, uncles, friends, and an amazing relationship with my husband, we made it work. Our kids seldom had to go to daycare; if they did, they went to a place where the people had similar values, similar discipline, and similar ideas. This is key in raising your children, exposing them to your values, emphasizing the traits they will carry on.

There wasn't always time to find reliable help at the office. One day I made a very scary call to the boss asking him to let me get rid of someone we had and hire someone who I knew would do things the right way... then I could spend more time with my babies. I had done my job, performed with honesty, courage, diligence, and communication, and my boss approved my request! You can't be afraid to ask to improve situations, if you don't ask, the answer will always be no. However be ready to make the boss happy with his decision to say yes.

I hired a young woman I knew who needed not only a job but also a life mentor. She did an amazing job. I became her boss, her mentor, and her friend, and we are friends to this day. She has taken steps out into the world that she acknowledges would not have been possible without my faith in her. I gave her a chance, an opportunity, and had confidence in her; she is grateful and so am I.

Even back then I knew in my heart that I wanted to set my sights on helping women to succeed. I believe women should look forward to a relationship with a man, not *need* a man to provide them with self-worth. Having your own money, goals, dreams, responsibilities, things to be accountable for, are parts of life a woman definitely ought to experience.

Personal Happiness Challenge:
What are your goals and dreams?

I have been blessed to have amazing women in my life, as you will see in a later chapter. But the women I chose to be around were those with confidence, desire, love, understanding, and goals. Not all women have that luxury, which is why I want this book to be a resource for women who don't, to help you feel love and confidence through the stories and guidance.

In 1997 I was given an offer to buy the company, a smoking deal to a then twenty-two-year-old with two little ones at home. I saw the potential, not only in the money but also in the chance to really make something of myself. We bought the business and operated under the original company name until April 2000, when I changed the name to Campbell Insurance Agency. I had that company until July 2009 when I started my own financial planning company, which I run today.

Until age thirty, it was an uphill battle (dancing backwards in high heels). Being in what truly is a man's industry, I was always being asked: "Whom did you inherit this from? Who is your dad? Do you work for him? How old are you? Do you even know what you're doing?" After being called young lady way too often, thirty was such a beautiful number.

*Value who you are,
even if someone else doesn't.*

—Author unknown

Chapter 2

Education Resources – Crucial and Available

W e need to learn—to get educated on how to most effectively use our passions and desires to become our best possible selves. Improving our skills and increasing our knowledge changes our lives for the better.

This education doesn't necessarily have to be a degree or a certification or a certificate or diploma to hang on the wall. Far more impressive is what we do in business on a daily basis. We live in a society in which people want to feel confident that you're well trained, and if in management, have the ability to train the people around you to work well under you.

When I looked at the community around me that had helped me grow into a prominent position as a businesswoman, wife, and mother, I was reminded that I cared about these people and about their well-being. I felt compassion. Honesty and compassion have always been traits I strive to keep strong within me. If you want people to want to do business with you, it's vital to form a trusting relationship.

Beyond that, you want to take steps necessary to better your current position, and seek additional education and training. You need to explore ideas regarding your long-term goals and do whatever it takes to continue serving to the best of your ability. Your goals need to include whether you want to be in a certain level of management, upper or middle, and decide the pace you want to adopt to get ahead. You need to decide on and plan for relaxation too, unless you really don't mind being a workaholic.

It's wisest to train employees well. You can become the person who's on vacation, spending money and spending time with her family, knowing she doesn't have to worry because an excellent, well-trained staff is taking care of the office.

Help the ones who have sincere ambition and who diligently serve the needs of your business. When you're in a position to see them succeed or move to a new level, there's nothing more gratifying than watching those around you blossom. People say there's room for growth and gain within any kind of employment, and that's true, but if you want to move up the ladder in substantial increments and get to where you notice a difference before years go by, you have to step out, step above, and step beyond.

> *Personal Happiness Challenge:*
> *What educational resources are you most*
> *in need of? Which educational resources*
> *are needed by members of your team*
> *(assistants, contractors, employees)?*

Chapter 3

Children Really Are the Future

*H*aving kids and having the ability to teach them as you grow; you discover more of who *you* are through them. It's about the stewardship of all things.

When I got married at age eighteen, my husband was twenty. We didn't plan to have our children young, but I learned that it was divine intervention—part of a larger plan. I realized all this much later in life. Part of the plan had me learn years later that I didn't know nearly as much at eighteen as I thought I did. Sure, I'd have told you then that I had it all figured out, but the truth is that I absolutely believe that God put me in a position to be a mother, wife, and business owner, blended all that together, and placed me right in the middle. A time arrived when I had to perform all those roles right—and I assure you, I did not do things right.

I had to reach out for help with my family. I needed to have people help me become a better businesswoman. I tried to be the rancher's wife that you read about in the magazines and see in the movies, but I was nowhere close—and to this day I'm still not.

Yes, I'm nowhere close, but I do have a great, unconditional love for my husband and my children.

Through all the teachings my family has instilled in me, I've come to realize that Trace and I have been placed as stewards of our children, to teach them correctly what not to do and to set an example of the right way to be.

I remember the day my son was born. During an

ultrasound prior to his birth, I looked at him and saw a little Campbell, a definitive view of the little Campbell boy, this Campbell boy that I was so ready to bring into the world!

I knew that I had to be the best mom I could be. It wasn't realistic to think I would be the "mother of the year" we all strive to be, but we're definitely all mothers of the year in our own ways—don't ever let anyone tell you or make you feel otherwise.

I knew that I had a big job, as my husband is an absolutely amazing man and I wanted both him and our baby boy to know right away that our son would be as amazing a man as his dad is.

After a day and a half of labor, Brad was born. Because of where Trace was standing, Brad's little arm flung out and slipped a high five on my husband! I will never forget the look on Trace's face, or the tears rolling down his cheeks, as we brought that young man into the world. From that day on, my hip son has looked up to his dad. Physically, emotionally, and spiritually he has shown great strides in becoming the fine young man that he is today. He observes my husband and sees what to do and also what not to do.

As a mother, I've been able to guide Brad. I've been able to sit down and say, "Talk to me about the pros and the cons, the good and the bad, the valleys and the peaks of what you see in this life."

We've had many, many discussions in which I have been able to show him things through his father's eyes, but his father could only show the interference that you sometimes have to run to clarify why dad does what he does. I tried, without being a helicopter mom, to point out all facets of the strength of a man through my eyes and my own strength.

My son is now twenty years old! Wise beyond his years, he's a young man whom children look up to, a young man whom older gentlemen want to converse with. He has a heart stronger, deeper, and more compassionate than any man his age I know. He's one who goes the extra mile for anyone around him, and unconditionally for his family. He is getting his strengths via the strength that Trace has shown him by example and from what Trace has shown him by physically doing things to teach him. By watching his father, Brad has found what to do and what not to do.

Part of being a good mom is being able to run interference between children and their fathers; being able to be the strength when it's needed, being able to be the one they can fall apart in front of.

Without undermining my husband's authority, I was able to help Brad understand why his dad expected so much of him. I helped our child understand why it is so important to be a good husband, a good father, a good friend, a good grandson, a good brother—we're all on this earth in a pattern, in a place, as part of a plan far bigger than each of us.

Brad has been a gift from God. He is all of the good and all of the bad of both my husband and me. It's so very important to both of us that we let Brad know how much he truly means to us. Sometimes time goes by without our expressing the extent of our love and appreciation—so we put it in writing for him.

A Letter to Brad

Dear Brad,

I hope you know how proud we are of you. The past eighteen years have flown by; we are really excited for you now that you get to become more independent. We remember how much we were looking forward to this time when we were your age.

We wanted to share some things with you that we learned as we grew older than you are now. I know that these might not seem important to you, and you can choose to ignore them if you want—that's your prerogative as an adult. However, knowing what we do now, we think that if we had known these things, life would have been a little bit easier on us.

You don't need to know what you want to do as your career, at least not right away. It's okay. We know a lot of people have been bugging you about this for several years. Adults you meet, school counselors with their aptitude tests, some of our friends, your aunts, uncles, and grandparents, all seem so curious about it. We also understand that it seems like you should have an answer to this stuff right now, but don't worry about it—you still have time.

Dad chose to stay on the ranch and help Papa, but in doing so gave up his desire for the military. Looking back, and being so political and patriotic, he regrets not having taken that step. Know that you have our unreserved support for whatever you choose to do, and don't be afraid to talk to us and brainstorm. I knew I wanted to work in sales and get married and start a family. We took a huge leap of faith at a young age and it was a very good decision. You have a lot of Mom's "people skills," and the world would be missing out if you didn't share the gift of your personality in whatever you choose to do. So, take your time and don't commit to anything too early.

Make some contacts, scope things out, ask questions. The folks you meet along your journey to being who you want to be will show you the good and bad in people; know that that's part of the deal, grow from that information, become better. Along these lines, do make friends with people. As an adult, you'll find value in your lifelong relationships, those you enjoy and even those you don't enjoy. You never know who'll be in a position to help you, or more important whom you'll be in a position to assist, down the road.

At this point in your life, we know you still view yourself as a kid, and you might feel like your views and opinions might not be valued. Wrong! Since you were a small child, you've had a way about you that amazed all of those around you and has made us gleam with pride. You are smart, you are informed, and your opinion does matter, so share it! Your love of life is far beyond many your age, so share your views and help those who struggle—they'll be excited at finding a kindred spirit, and may become some of your first "grown-up" friends.

When you have the opportunity, travel. Take advantage of seeing new places and meeting new people; there's a big world out there, don't be afraid to explore it. Prepare for the types of interactions you'll have, both with locals and with other travelers. Travel teaches self-reliance, getting out of your comfort zone, how to manage money, and a bunch *of other stuff. If you decide you want to ranch, it'll definitely be there when you get back from wherever you've been, and you'll have lots more material for your résumé with your dad.*

We've already dealt with this on multiple fronts, we think, but it bears repeating: Don't lock yourself into stuff, especially while you're young. Take a lot of time to consider any big purchases or decisions from all angles. Commitment is great, but make sure you really know what you're committing to. If you're worried, ask several people you trust what they think about it, explain your logic, and see if you've forgotten to consider any aspects of the issue. We don't want you to repeat our mistakes, but we want you to grow from them. Popularity is a contest you don't have to deal with anymore. You were popular, but that's not going to get you many places once you leave high school. Check your ego at the door, just relax and be yourself.

Find something you enjoy and make a hobby of it. You'll spend many years of your life working, so make sure to also find something you can enjoy doing for the rest of your life that isn't work related. You'll be happiest with it if it's something you can do that helps other people. Not on the grand scale of Helping People, but if it brings enjoyment to those around you, that's something you can genuinely be proud of.

Whatever you choose for a career shouldn't seem like "work." We've probably said this to you before, but finding what you love to do doesn't mean that everything involved with it is always smooth sailing. There will be parts of any task that you don't necessarily enjoy; however, those parts shouldn't outweigh what you do enjoy about it. Have a virtual scale in your mind with everything you don't like on one side and everything you enjoy on the other. If the good outweighs the bad, then keep that in mind when you need to do the bad stuff. It'll motivate you to get through it so you can do something fun. If the bad outweighs the good, then it's time to find something else to do. This applies to everything in life. If a book you're reading isn't any good, then put it down. If you don't enjoy a movie that everyone says you should, who cares? Life is too short to waste it on doing things you should do, rather than things you want to do—with obvious exceptions, like feeding your family.

Well, if you've gotten to the end of this, you've got more discipline than we had at your age, but neither of us has ever doubted that. There are other things we'd like to tell you, and don't worry, we will, but they're not coming to mind at the moment. We hope this has been helpful, and not just in a "We're older than you and we know more" sense. We hope that it's stimulated you to think more about your preconceptions. Always be asking questions. If something doesn't seem right to you, whatever it is, don't be afraid to ask yourself why. And, most important, don't be afraid to make mistakes. It happens to everyone, and you're young enough that you've got a ton of time to correct any that you make. We love you so very much and are so very proud of you.

Unconditionally,
Mom & Dad

There are several things to pull from the letter above and share with your kids. Sometimes having some references in writing for them does a lot of good; it's not just going in one ear and out the other.

Personal Happiness Challenge:
Take a moment to craft a letter you
would like to give to a loved one in
your life. Why is this person important
to you? What message would you most
want to convey to this person?

Young Brad and Tracee.

Our daughter, Tracee, is a blessing beyond measure. She came into this world far faster than our son did. We lived in a rural area where it took an hour and a half to get to the hospital. Having a baby was no exception. She came into this world quickly and ready to take it all on. Tracee has a passion for children and animals, and a huge love for her family and friends. She has grown up living on the ranch learning love, respect, and admiration for all those around her and for animals. I've always felt that you can tell a lot about people by the way they treat children and animals, and this young lady is the essence of compassion.

She has watched me and has learned how to talk to people, learned how to deal with people, learned that sometimes saying how you feel is not good. To her friends she's a very likable, lovable, intelligent, beautiful young lady. She speaks her mind without question. We live in a society in which some people think, in an old-fashioned sense, that women have their place. Tracee is a young lady who will make her place based on example.

You have to teach your children, especially the young women in your life—daughters, nieces, cousins, and friends—that women have not only an important place in this world but also have the most important job in the world. Being a mother is the lowest-paid but most-needed, valuable job to do correctly and wisely.

You can be good at everything you do, but if you're not a good mother and aren't setting a good example, you've accomplished nothing. We women are bringing into this world women who must be strong physically, emotionally, and spiritually, and must realize the importance of developing these strengths.

Reading the feelings Tracee expressed in her message below gave me a wonderful feeling that, yes, my making my children top priority helped both of them develop into the amazing young adults that our planet needs more of.

I am so proud of both Tracee and Brad, and thankful that Trace and I gave so much thought and effort to learning and putting to use all the tools we could for effective parenting. I am also grateful that we did our best to surround our children with people who shared our morals and had the best interests of our children in mind.

Tracee's Grateful Message

I have been blessed with amazing people in my life. I could not imagine having a more quality set of friends and family. The support and love I have gotten throughout the years is amazing.

Mom, you are my inspiration. You have taught me so much about life and what it means to love unconditionally. I will forever cherish the time spent with you. I am going to miss spending my days with you, whether trying out new Pinterest ideas or just watching movies. Because of you I am a stronger, more understanding person.

Daddy, I love you so much. You are the most amazing person in my life. I now know that life is tough and the struggles only make the journey worth it. I wouldn't trade a hot day building fences with you for anything. I will forever be your little girl; never forget that you are my reason to be the best that I can be.

Papa John, you have been my biggest fan throughout life, and I can't think of anyone else I would want behind me through everything. Thank you for always cheering me on and for believing in me in whatever I may be doing.

My Shash, I don't know where to start. The worst part about all of this is to know that I will be hundreds of miles away from you. You have taught me how to show empathy toward those who need it most. It's the little things that you have said and done over the years that make my memories amazing. The greatest title I own is being your granddaughter, and I wouldn't change that for the world!

Papa Lyman and Grandma Norma, thank you both for taking care of me as a child and letting me spend the night. I know I was not your favorite bed partner, but I enjoyed it. The time I spent with you is something I have treasured throughout the years.

Uncle Moe, thank you for always supporting me in everything I do. I have really enjoyed growing up *with you, and I am so grateful that I got to spend a lot of my childhood with you. I am going to miss you while I'm at college.*

Uncle Mike, thank you for being my coach not only in high school basketball but also for being my coach in life. When I had a bad attitude and no will to try, you always made me want to work harder, even at things I hated. I don't know how you do it, but I am so glad you do.

Aunt Mona, you are my rock. You probably don't know how much you mean to me, and I don't know if I could ever show you. I feel like I have to tell you all my stories, and I search for your advice. You would be amazed at how much I have learned from you and put to use without your knowing. You are a blessing, and I don't know what I am going to do without you keeping me on track in college.

Brad, thanks for being so entertaining and keeping me on my toes. Living with you has been so much fun; you're the best big brother ever. Thank you for teaching me so many important life lessons. I don't even know how I am going to live without you next year.

Tracee and Brad celebrating victory and loss together.

Chapter 4

Want a Man,
Not Need a Man!

*I*t's important for young women to understand that society has a narrow notion of how and where women are supposed to be. We live in a time when women can be highly successful as mothers, wives, business owners, employees, managers, and more. There's a saying about dancing backwards in high heels—Fred Astaire was touted as the amazing dancer, but it was Ginger Rogers who danced backwards and in high heels.

One of the most important lessons for me to teach my daughter was that she'd eventually have to fight an uphill battle. If you fight it with grace, dignity, honesty, and compassion, there is no reason in the world that you can't sit in any position a man might hold.

Daughter Tracee has a very liberal mindset in that respect; she holds no judgment and feels that everyone is free to be who she wants to be. If she's not hurting anyone, that's not a problem. She was raised in a very conservative household. Now that she's grown up, she has taught me as a mother to take a step back and reevaluate people, always giving them the benefit of the doubt.

Sis never turns her back on anyone who needs help; she's always reaching out to lend a hand. The saying "Never look down on someone unless you're helping them up" could not be truer about this young lady's philosophy.

Tracee has learned to know what might be most important to be concerned about from my husband and through me—whether it is an animal that's sick and struggling or a friend in need of a cup of coffee and a chocolate doughnut and a good cry.

She knows the necessity of helping those around her. She helped with her grandmothers as they were dying; she has always reached out to help. She has cuddled and coddled and wrapped her loving arms around everyone in need.

And I'm so proud to say she has learned this from the example we set, and when I say example we set, it's also an example set by you! By reading this book, you prepare yourself to help your daughters, your sons, your sisters, your cousins, your aunts — to become the very best they can be. And to help yourself be the best you can be too!

Chapter 5

Keys to Strong Marriages and Partnerships

*M*arried life or partnership isn't about always getting your way, always being right, or always making the right decisions. Oh, sure, it may appear that way in the movies we see or the love stories we read, but in fact it's quite the opposite. In the real world it's a lot of work, a lot of give and take. It's all about positive compromise. It's true that happiness is a journey not a destination.

When it comes to the traditional roles of men and women, being an independent woman entails obligations. It's easy to want to be in charge and call the shots, but in reality the responsibilities of "being in charge" must be shared to generate true equality.

✦ Who is the breadwinner, and does it matter? Who's making the most money, and does it matter? Is your own level of personal and business success any more important than your life partner's?

✦ Giving credit where credit is due works both ways.

✦ Know what you can and can't control, and accept both.

✦ Contribute something wherever you can. Ask yourself *do I love this person enough to make this work?* If the answer is yes, then learn what you have to do.

+ Let your partner lead the way. Maybe it's the same checking account, but let him pick up the check.

+ Talk about financial decisions; you wouldn't feel good if you were put in second place. You have to be partners on level ground.

Personal Happiness Challenge:
Do you have a life partner? If so, what are three positive actions you commit to taking over the next 90 days to strengthen your relationship with your partner?

Other Challenges

Every one of us has a family member, a spouse, or a friend who struggles with addiction, whether to a substance or to behaviors. Have you triggered them? Can you fix them? What is your role in their challenge?

You have to find a balance between learning how to fix what's your fault and letting go of the guilt over what had nothing to do with you.

It wasn't until I reached out for professional help that I could do this. Sometimes you have to help work toward a solution even if the addicted person is unwilling to. It would have been really easy to try and fix it all myself, read the Bible and read devotionals, but sometimes that's not enough. Take the initiative to use all your best resources and get the help that will guide you through the journey; we are not able to make all the transitions in our lives alone.

How in life can you show your kids and your peers that it's important to have someone stand beside you, not in front of you or behind you?

It wasn't until my kids were grown that they said to me, "Thank you for sticking around, thank you for not giving up, thank you for teaching us that just because people make poor decisions or have addictions, that doesn't necessarily make them bad people."

Wow! I never even realized that they were watching.

Wendy and Trace.

Chapter 6

The Beauty of Friendship

riends come in all shapes, sizes, and levels of income, and they all fill voids in our lives. Why do we sometimes try too damn hard to impress them? What decisions do we make that will ultimately affect our marriage or partnership just to impress them? Who are Mr. and Mrs. Jones that we have that need to keep up with them, anyway?

Over the years our circle of friends has grown, dwindled, changed, etc. The Joneses are building a house, so should we do that? And then, when we each have parties, can we show them how well we're doing? A new car in the store's parking lot—whose is it? I wonder if they financed it? Hmm, they must be doing well. Should we upgrade? Designer clothes, fancy labels, top-dollar wine or Scotch—would you drink that if it were just you and your partner at home in your sweats?

Must have acrylic nails even though I can't type with them; look how sophisticated they look, show off that diamond a little better don't you think? Oh, and what about trading in and upgrading rings to show off on your hand wrapped around that wineglass?

Whom am I doing this for? Who is Mrs. Jones again? Does she notice? Is she doing the same thing? Does she even care about me or who I am? Do I really care what she thinks?

Become Mrs. Jones by being the real deal, the friend who loves and supports unconditionally, the one whom other ladies look up to and say, "She's happy with herself, she loves herself and others, and doesn't worry about what others think of her. I want to be like that."

She carries herself with strength and dignity and lives without fear of the future (Proverbs 31).

These habits of trying to impress those around you are destructive, exhausting, expensive, and not even enjoyable, so why do we do it? Whom are we trying to impress?

Do you like who you are? Do your real friends care about all that pretentious nonsense? Are you buying their acceptance or friendship? Do they sit around trying to figure out how to impress you?

Girl, who has time for that—there's stuff to be done! You have a family to take care of, a husband to amaze, and kids to set an example for; do you want them acting this showy way? At the end of the day, no one cares—that's right, no one cares.

Those who matter don't mind. Throw on your lounge clothes, grab some pastries, and go sit and visit with your real best friend. Betcha she'll let you in. And if you show up unexpectedly, I bet her hair's in a headband and she's got no makeup on. Will you care?

Chapter 7

Battles/Wars/
Challenges/Conquests

*W*hat is important enough to fight over? When do you fight? When do you argue? When should you keep your mouth shut, and when should you trudge ahead?

Life as a woman is complicated; we spend much of our time finding solutions to problems. These problems can be associated with our husbands, our families, our jobs, the weekly sale at the grocery store, the car pool, the school, and our own emotions. Do we *ever* say no? If we do, are we saying no to the things we should be saying yes to?

What is Important?

1. Your children

2. Your husband

3. Your health

4. Your finances

5. Your happiness

6. Your faith

What do you put first and why? Make a list, pros on one side and cons on the other. Determine which obstacles you need to conquer, which battles on your list you need to win to ultimately succeed.

The war lets us know what matters. What did I do to be the person I've become? Am I happy with what I see? What might I have done differently?

When you are gone, what will your family and friends remember about you? What mattered, what didn't? There's a popular saying: "You won't remember what I said, but you will long remember how I made you feel."

What if you could shift gears right now and say, "I am going to make a conscious effort to _____, and the end result will be _____? You can, right this minute, shift those gears and answer that question. Go ahead.

My kids are grown. I was there for all the Little League, church programs, bake sales, school plays, middle school and high school sports, summer recreation leagues, and fundraisers. I was that mom who said, "I can do it all" and I did—because I managed and controlled what I was willing to put my energy into, and let go of what I chose to let someone else handle. Everyday battles became easier. I was there for my kids, and I feel like I still missed out, but at the end of the day, they knew that my heart was with them and that they could always depend on me.

Sure, I gave up other things, the social time with the ladies... who are they again? And the parties on the weekends with the other couples, but I found my purpose within those battlefields. I could set an example, show other moms what they were missing, and fill in when moms who wanted to be there couldn't. I hope I made a difference in all those people's lives. I structured my battles to work toward winning the war, the challenge of making a good life. You have to consider doing the same.

Chapter 8

Sundays in
Sweatpants

*A*s I became an adult and had a family, some of my favorite times have been our Sundays in our loungewear. Both Trace and I were raised in church. His family is devout Pentecostal, and my mom raised us in a Baptist church. My dad joined us only for programs or holidays, but never discouraged us from going.

Around the age of sixteen, it was becoming clear to me while dating that the things I enjoyed doing that were totally harmless were completely frowned upon by the respective church families I had been raised in. Dancing was a big one. I loved to dance, and nothing was ever done before, during, or after dances that I couldn't and didn't do anyway.

That's when I started seeing the hypocrisy of it all. I continued to attend church occasionally, as I had developed a relationship with God. I acknowledged, however, that I questioned the manmade, organized side of religion.

When we married, the Baptist pastor of the church we attended performed our ceremony. We spent some time with him prior to the wedding, and he said something that I will never forget, "Go with God in your lives; only you will know as a couple where you will go." He married us in a beautiful Colorado July ceremony.

When we had children we put them in AWANA, a children's ministry that serves more than a hundred denominations. It's a faith-based after-school program. Uncle Moe, one of the most incredible, most righteous men I know, was a leader, a leader in life, love, and God. He helped guide our kids to their relationship with God, and to be goodhearted, good human beings.

No question about it: children are molded by their environment, and it was important to us that we teach our kids about God and the difference between God and Church. Uncle Moe and AWANA emphasized that.

On 9/11, our daughter was five and our son was six, and we sat out on the deck with them and talked to them that night about what had happened—as much as children that age could digest. The conversation led me to pray that night that we as parents were giving them the right guidance in their relationship with God. Were we doing enough? What if our children were ever in a situation in which they needed to know how to pray? Were they doing it right? If their lives were to be taken, would they go to Heaven? Did Heaven exist? This was a question that I had never really expressed between Trace and me, but this was different, these were my precious little ones. Will we reunite again when death separates us?

It was at that time that I read Rick Warren's *The Purpose Driven Life* and was taken to a place where I really found that Scripture was a guide. I believe in God and I believe in God's teaching, not man's teaching. I have tried hard to live my life in a way that people who know me sense my faith in God, and the most important example is to my children in every phase of their lives.

Sundays at our house have been that sanctuary for us as we raised our children, when the kids were little and snuggled up in the blankets to watch cartoons or read, the later years when football was fun for them to watch with Dad, and as teenagers when their friends would come over just to "hang out." And now that they're grown, we cherish a day with no schedule, no agenda, just each other. Now that the kids are adults and we have an empty nest, things are no different. Sunday is our day to regroup, relax, and remind ourselves of all our blessings. There are always a few snacks and an open dialog, rest, and peace within our refuge. We all have to reach out to where we find our peace, our belief, and our sanctuary. For you, is that home with you in your sweatpants?

So many things you've found and will find in this book have a reference to Scripture. I believe in God, I believe not only in what I have been taught but also in what I have reached out to learn.

It is our responsibility as moms, wives, friends, sisters, daughters etc., to teach through example and to share what works and what doesn't.

Don't let all you know be all you know.

Chapter 9

My Grandmothers' Legacies

*T*his chapter is about learning to let go and the loss of one's support system through death—all of which I learned from the women who molded me.

Grandma Midge

When my Grandma Midge reached the point when she could no longer see, there was something about my husband's rough, rugged hands that made her just hold them and visit with him as she rubbed his hands. She would always say, "Honey, you are working so hard, I can tell." She knew Trace by his hands, and never missed a time to tell him what a hardworking man he was.

It was at that time that I found this poem. It said so much to me—not only about the truth but also about Grandma Midge and how all her life was, but it speaks, too, about how we all hold our "wear and tear" in our appearance.

*Have you ever looked
at Grandma Midge's hands?*

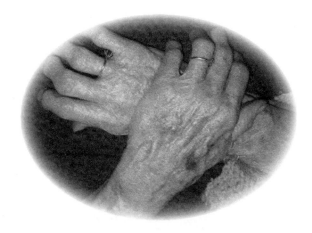

I mean, really looked at her hands?

Stop and think for a moment about the hands of this woman and how they have served her through the years. These hands, though wrinkled, shriveled, and weak, have been mighty tools she used throughout her life to reach out to grab and embrace life.

They braced her and caught her fall when she was a toddler and crashed upon the floor. They put food in her mouth and clothes on her back.

When she was a child, her mother taught her to fold them in prayer. Those hands tied her shoes and put on her boots. They held Grandpa, and they wiped her tears when she cried. They have been dirty, scraped and raw, swollen and bent. They were uneasy and clumsy when she tried to hold her newborn children. Decorated by her wedding band, they showed the world she was married and loved.

They trembled and shook when she buried her parents and her spouse. They have held our children and each of us; they consoled neighbors, and shook in fists of anger when she didn't understand. They have covered her face, combed her hair, and washed and cleansed the rest of her body. They have been sticky and wet, bent and broken, dried and raw. And to this day when not much of anything on her works real well, these hands hold her up, lay her down, and again continue to fold in prayer.

These hands are the mark of where she has been and the ruggedness of life. But more important, these are the hands that God will take when He reaches out to lead her back home. And with her hands, He will lift her to His side. There she will use those hands to touch the face of Christ. She will never look at her hands the same way again. As life goes on for each of us, when our hands are hurt or sore, or when we stroke the faces of our children and husband, it is only natural that we think of Grandma, and all the love placed in her hands.

Grandma Jane

All who have socialized with the Royer family know that we never do things with just a few people around, or a little food; it's always a lot of people and a lot of food.

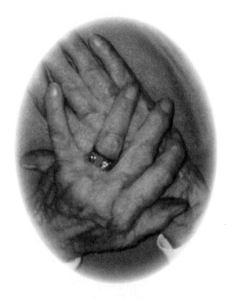

The last day of Grandma Jane's life was no exception. The house was jam-packed, loud, and bustling with utter chaos. Counters were covered with wonderful foods, and the special occasion was simply a family gathering. The only unusual thing was that we were saying goodbye to the matriarch of our family, not scooting her up to the table to finish off the night playing poker.

She would often look around at the chaos and noise, and if you asked her, "Grandma, are you responsible for all these people?" she would smile and say, "Why, yes I am."

Not many kids can say that their ninety-seven-year-old grandmother was sitting in the end zone when they ran or threw a touchdown, or that she sat in the bleachers when the basketball or volleyball games were going on, but ours could, even when it meant the boys would bring her down or up the stairs in a chair to make sure she was able to be seated. A smile would come across her face when we would say, "That was your grandson or granddaughter who just made that play," and she would say, "Well, of course it was." She not only saw what was going on but she felt the pride in her heart for all of our successes and theirs, both little and big.

Things I learned from Grandma Jane that I would like to share:

✦ She taught me that just because two people argue doesn't mean that they don't love each other, and just because they don't argue doesn't mean they do.

✦ There will be friends and family who will hurt you, and that's okay; you have to forgive them. Only they know their internal struggles, and we should be big enough inside to realize that.

✦ It isn't always enough to be forgiven by others; sometimes you have to forgive yourself.

✦ She taught me that every woman should have several things: A youth that she is content to leave behind; a past juicy enough to look forward to retelling in her old age; a feeling of control of her own destiny; an ability to fall in love without losing her personal identity, and the ability to know when to try harder and when to walk away.

✦ She showed me that there were those whom I could trust and those whom I couldn't, and that I mustn't take that fact personally.

✦ She showed me that when my heart needed soothing, it didn't matter if it was on my best friend's couch, in a quiet room, or sitting in the recliner in her living room—it was important to have the ability to sit and be myself at each.

✦ She taught me that life isn't always fair but it is always good.

✦ And that it's okay to agree to disagree and not compare yourself to others—since you have no idea what their life's journey is all about.

✦ That no matter how good or how bad a situation is, it will change; that if we put all of our worries in a pile and could see everyone else's, we would ask for our own back.

+ She taught me that maturity has more to do with what types of experiences you have had and what you learned from them, not how many birthdays you've celebrated.

+ And that while our background and circumstances may have influenced who we are, only we are responsible for whom we become.

In her final days I found that two people could look at the same thing and see things completely differently, whether it was religion, politics, faith, or how to prepare a bowl of soup. Realizing that is how we grow, change, understand, and believe. And how our lives can be changed in a matter of hours.

She taught me that you can keep going long after you think you can't, and that it is so very important to spend time with loved ones and say loving words, as one day it will be the last time you see them. Tomorrow is not promised to any of us, regardless of our age. Your job won't take care of you when you're sick, your family will, so stay in touch. I encourage you to hold your loved ones tight, take the time for that glass of iced tea and visit; you will be amazed at what you will learn, not only about the family or friend you're visiting with but what you'll learn about yourself. I know without a doubt that my lifetime with Grandma Jane and Grandma Midge has made me the person I want to be.

I am grateful to both of my grandmas for helping me finally realize that it's okay to burn the candles, use the good sheets, and use the fancy dishes. Every day is a special occasion, so why should we wait to say, use, and do the things we usually save for later?

Life was so different for my grandmothers. Knowing them as a child, a young adult, and a married adult, they both taught me so much. They died within two years of each other, in the loving arms of our family. I was blessed to be there until the end came for each of them. As the final breaths and all signs of life left their bodies, the question again arose for me: Will we see each other after death separates us?

I was able to hold their hands, and kiss their cheeks with calm assurance that yes, I would see them again. Until that time, they will be my guardian angels. I often go to the local cemetery where they, along with my grandfathers, are laid to rest. I sit and talk to them, and somehow feel the answers to my questions, or maybe it is reassurance on decisions I have to make. All I am and hope to be are equal parts of my beloved grandmothers.

My relationship with daughter Sis has developed into a friendship that I struggle to put into words. She is an amazing young woman. I watched as my mother, aunt, and cousin had the privilege, yes privilege, of taking care of my grandmothers in their final years. My hope, my wish, my desire, is that I can live my life in a way that when the time comes for my care I can count on Tracee to be there every step of the way. I want her to know, the day you see I'm getting old, I ask you to please be patient, but most of all, try to understand what I'm going through.

If when we talk, I repeat the same thing a thousand times, don't interrupt to say, "You said the same thing a minute ago." Just listen, please. Try to remember the times when you were little and I would read the same story to you night after night until you fell asleep.

When I don't want to take a bath, don't be angry and don't embarrass me. Remember when you were just a girl and I had to run after you, trying to get you to take a shower?

When you see how ignorant I am when it comes to new technology, give me the time to learn and don't look at me in that condescending way. Remember, honey, I patiently taught you how to do many things like eat appropriately, get dressed, comb your hair, and deal with life's everyday issues. The day you see I'm getting old, I ask you to please be patient, but most of all, try to understand what I'm going through.

If I occasionally lose track of what we're talking about, give me time to remember, and if I can't, don't be nervous, impatient, or arrogant. Just know in your heart that the most important thing for me is to be with you.

And when my old, tired legs don't let me move as quickly as before, give me your hand the same way that I offered mine to you when you first walked.

When those days come, don't feel sad... just be with me, and understand me while I get to the end of my life with love.

I'll cherish and thank you for the gift of time and joy we shared. With a big smile and the huge love I've always had for you, I just want to say, I love you... my darling daughter."
—Author Unknown

Personal Happiness Challenge:
Who has left you a legacy? How could you ever acknowledge or repay that gift?

Chapter 10

Obstacles to Success

A Few Fun Facts

+ If you never ask, the answer will always be no.

+ If you don't take steps forward you will always be in the same place.

+ If you don't go after what you want, you will never get it!

*W*asting time feeling sorry for yourself is a bad idea. You don't see mentally strong people feel sorry for themselves or dwell on the way they've been treated—or mistreated. They have learned to take responsibility for their actions and be accountable for all they do. You don't hear them saying, "Life isn't fair." They rise up and move on from trying circumstances with self-awareness and gratitude, thankful for the lessons learned. When a situation turns out badly, they respond with phrases such as "Oh, well" or "Moving on"... and not only do they say that, they believe it.

Giving Away Your Power

Strong women avoid giving others the power to make them feel inferior or bad. They understand they are in control of their actions and emotions. They know their strength lies in their ability to manage the way they respond. They not only say this but they put it to work.

You must never shy away from change. Strong women embrace change and welcome challenge. There is a German proverb that says, "Fear makes the wolf bigger than he is." Their biggest fear, if they have one, is not of the unknown but of becoming complacent and stagnant. An environment of change and even uncertainty can energize a mentally strong woman and bring out her best.

A Carrot, an Egg and a Cup of Coffee

You will never look at a cup of coffee the same way again.

A young woman went to her mother and told her about her life and how things were so hard for her. She didn't know how she was going to make it and wanted to give up, tired of fighting and struggling. It seemed that as one problem was solved, a new one arose.

Her mother took her to the kitchen. She filled three pots with water and placed each over a high flame. Soon the pots came to boil. In the first she placed carrots, in the second she placed eggs, and in the last she placed ground coffee beans. She let them sit and boil without saying a word, and after about twenty minutes she turned off the burners. She fished the carrots out and placed them in a bowl. She pulled the eggs out and placed them in a bowl. Then she ladled out the coffee and placed it in a bowl. Turning to her daughter, she said, "Tell me what you see."

"Carrots, eggs, and coffee," she replied.

Her mother brought her closer and asked her to feel the carrots. She did and noted that they were soft. The mother then asked the daughter to take an egg and break it. After pulling off the shell, she observed the hardboiled egg.

Finally, the mother asked the daughter to sip the coffee. The daughter smiled at its rich flavor, and then asked, "What does it mean, Mother?"

Her mother explained that each of these objects had faced the same adversity: Boiling water. Each reacted differently. The carrot went in strong, hard, and unrelenting, but after being subjected to the boiling water, it softened and became weak. The egg had been fragile. Its thin outer shell had protected its liquid interior, but after sitting through the boiling water, its inside became hardened. The ground coffee beans were unique, however. After they sat in the boiling water, they had changed the water.

"Which are you?" she asked her daughter. "When adversity knocks on your door, how do you respond? Are you a carrot, an egg, or a coffee bean?

Think of this: Which am I? Am I the carrot that seems strong, but with pain and adversity do I wilt and become soft and lose my strength?

Am I the egg that starts with a malleable heart but changes with the heat? Did I have a fluid spirit, but after a death, a breakup, a financial hardship, or some other trial, have I become hardened and stiff? Does my shell look the same, but on the inside am I bitter and tough with a stiff spirit and hardened heart?

Or am I like the coffee bean, which actually changes the hot water in the very circumstance that brings the pain. When the water gets hot, it releases the fragrance and flavor. If you are like the bean, when things are at their worst, you get better and change the situation around you.

When the hour is the darkest and trials are their greatest, do you elevate yourself to another level? How do you handle adversity? Are you a carrot, an egg, or a coffee bean?

May you have enough happiness to make you sweet, enough trials to make you strong, enough sorrow to keep you human, and enough hope to make you happy.

The happiest of people don't necessarily have the best of everything; they just make the most of everything that comes their way. The brightest future will always be based on a forgotten past; you can't go forward in life until you let go of your past failures and heartaches.

> *When you were born, you were crying and everyone around you was smiling.*
>
> *Live your life so at the end, you're the one who is smiling and everyone around you is crying.*
>
> —Author unknown

Try not to waste energy on things you can't control. Strong women don't complain (much) about bad traffic, lost luggage, or especially about other people; they recognize that all of these things are generally beyond their control. In a bad situation, they recognize that the one thing they can always control is their own attitude and response.

Don't worry about pleasing others. A strong woman makes a point to be kind and fair and to please others where appropriate, but is not afraid to speak up. She is able to withstand the possibility that someone will get upset with what she says or does; she understands that that's part of the deal, and she will navigate the situation with grace and with class. Remember that example you are setting.

A strong woman is willing to take calculated risks. This is entirely different from jumping headfirst into a foolish venture. With mental strength, an individual can weigh the risks and benefits thoroughly. Your pros and cons list should also follow this part of your life, weighing what you're planning and why. Make your decisions based on the list.

Strong women enjoy and even long for the time they spend alone. They use their downtime to reflect, to plan, and to be productive. Most important, they don't depend on others to determine their happiness and mood. Strong women can be happy with others around them and they can also be happy by themselves.

It's not helpful to dwell on the past—it's over. Don't get me wrong, there is strength in acknowledging what we've been through, and especially the things we learned, but a strong woman is able to avoid doing those wrong things again, and she can invest the majority of her energy in creating a better present and future. Try not to make the same mistakes over and over. We all know the definition of insanity, right? It's when we perform the same actions again and again while hoping for a different and better outcome than we've gotten before. A strong woman accepts full responsibility for past behavior and is willing to learn from her mistakes. Research shows that the ability to be self-reflective in an accurate and productive way is one of the greatest strengths of spectacularly successful executives and entrepreneurs.

Don't Resent Other People's Success. It takes strength of character to feel genuine joy and excitement for other people's success. People say, "Oh, I am so happy for you." Do they mean it? Do you mean it when you say the same thing? Strong women have this ability. They don't become jealous or resentful when others succeed, but take careful notes on what the successful individual did well. They are willing to work hard for their own chance at success, without relying on shortcuts. A grateful heart cannot be a jealous heart, and this is a good thing.

Don't Give Up After You Don't Succeed

In my office I have a sign that I found on Facebook. It says:

Optimist
Someone who figures that taking a step backward
After taking a step forward is not a disaster...
It's more like a cha-cha.

Every failure is a chance to improve. Some of the greatest entrepreneurs are willing to admit that their early efforts brought many failures. Strong women are willing to fail again and again if necessary, as long as the learning experience from every failure brings them closer to their ultimate goal.

Do you feel the world owes you anything? Particularly in the current economy, executives and employees at every level are realizing that the world does not owe them a salary, a benefits package, or a comfortable life, regardless of their preparation and schooling. Strong women enter the world prepared to work and succeed on their own merits, at every stage of the game. The fact that you are reading this book is a great indicator of your desire for success. Personal gratification, there's nothing better!

It's unrealistic to expect immediate results. Whether it's a workout plan, a nutritional regimen, or starting a business, strong women are "in it for the long haul." They know better than to expect immediate results. They apply their energy and time in measured doses, and they celebrate each milestone and increment of success along the way. They have their own stamina—staying power—and they understand that great things take time. Rome wasn't built in a day.

Steve Jobs said, "The only way to do great work is to love what you do, if you haven't found it yet keep looking, don't settle, as with all matters of the heart, you will know when you find it."

Take advantage of resources—they are all around you.

Personal Happiness Challenge:
Do you see yourself today as a "strong woman?" If so, how would you describe yourself? If not, what would have to change before you could begin envisioning yourself as a "strong woman?"
When do you want to start?

Chapter 11

What Doesn't Kill Us Makes Us Stronger

*F*ound written on the wall in Mother Teresa's home for children in Calcutta:

People are often unreasonable, irrational, and self-centered. Forgive them anyway.

If you are kind, people may accuse you of selfish, ulterior motives. Be kind anyway.

If you are successful, you will win some unfaithful friends and some genuine enemies.

Succeed anyway.

If you are honest and sincere people may deceive you.

Be honest and sincere anyway.

What you spend years creating, others could destroy overnight. Create anyway.

If you find serenity and happiness, some may be jealous. Be happy anyway.

The good you do today will often be forgotten. Do good anyway.

Give the best you have, and it will never be enough. Give your best anyway.

In the final analysis, it is between you and God.

It was never between you and them anyway.

I have done many things wrong but have done my best to learn from those things. Life is a journey, people are put into our lives and our paths to show us what to do, what not to do, whom to aspire to be, and whom we would never want to be like. And the really cool thing is that we as women have the innate ability to choose, to recreate ourselves, and be examples of the ideal woman. But are we? Think back to the situations in your life that made you change something. Maybe it was a thought process, maybe it was the way you verbalize your thoughts. What is it about your environment that is molding you? Are those things that you're proud of? Thankful for? Ashamed of?

Have there been times in your life when you thought *there is no possible way I am going to make it through this?* Did you make it through? How? Those are strengths—are you building on them?

You might be in a position where you think *it takes all I have to just get through my day.* Mentally, physically, emotionally, spiritually, financially, the reality is that sometimes, when we feel we have so little in one or more of these areas, it actually means we have the most to give. The best part of your life will be in the small nameless moments you spend smiling with someone who matters to you. I've often thought *when my family stands around my grave, what will they say?*

It's so hard to stay focused and stay positive. I know that. God knows I've struggled with this same battle, and that was part of my motivation to write this book, to pull together all the things that kept me going. I have often prayed in pure exhaustion, "God, I don't mean to complain, I know there are so many who are dealing with so much more than I am, and so many who are far less fortunate, but God, I'm running on empty. I feel like I have nothing left, nothing to give to my kids, my husband, my job. God, I know you expect more from me. I expect more from me. I know what strength you have given me, and God, I am thankful. I know that I have your strength to rely on, and I am falling on your mercy to build me back up. I know you are the God that never tires, so God, help me to rest in your strength tonight and help me do it all again tomorrow." I have learned the hard way that sometimes God calms the storm and sometimes He lets the storm rage and He calms his child. Thanks be to God.

There are references throughout this book. Feel free to use them, reach out to find your own sources of wisdom. Make a reference booklet for yourself. Keep it close to you, refer back, learn, and grow!

> *The most important thing is to enjoy your life — to be happy — it's all that matters.*
> — Audrey Hepburn

Chapter 12

What I Want the Women in My Life to Know

*L*isten up ladies, this is something you all need to know: Have a positive self-image; this assures power, strength, ability, and value. The verse below can help you to conquer your goals and allow you to fearlessly pursue your biggest dreams.

Proverbs 31, Epilogue: The Wife of Noble Character

10 A wife of noble character who can find?
   She is worth far more than rubies.

11 Her husband has full confidence in her
   and lacks nothing of value.

12 She brings him good, not harm,
   all the days of her life.

13 She selects wool and flax
   and works with eager hands.

14 She is like the merchant ships,
   bringing her food from afar.

15 She gets up while it is still night;
   she provides food for her family
   and portions for her female servants.

16 She considers a field and buys it;
   out of her earnings she plants a vineyard.

17 She sets about her work vigorously;
   her arms are strong for her tasks.

18 She sees that her trading is profitable,
   and her lamp does not go out at night.

19 In her hand she holds the distaff
   and grasps the spindle with her fingers.

20 She opens her arms to the poor
   and extends her hands to the needy.

21 When it snows, she has no fear for her household;
   for all of them are clothed in scarlet.

22 She makes coverings for her bed;
   she is clothed in fine linen and purple.

23 Her husband is respected at the city gate,
   where he takes his seat among the elders of the
   land.

24 She makes linen garments and sells them,
   and supplies the merchants with sashes.

25 She is clothed with strength and dignity;
   she can laugh at the days to come.

26 She speaks with wisdom,
   and faithful instruction is on her tongue.

27 She watches over the affairs of her household
   and does not eat the bread of idleness.

28 Her children arise and call her blessed;
   her husband also, and he praises her:

29 "Many women do noble things,
   but you surpass them all."

30 Charm is deceptive, and beauty is fleeting;
   but a woman who fears the Lord is to be praised.

31 Honor her for all that her hands have done,
   and let her works bring her praise at the city gate.

What all young women in our lives need to know—and
it's up to us to remind them:

> *Smart and strong are the new beautiful, so it is said.*
> *Friends are invaluable, they are trusting and loyal,*
> *they will stick with you through good times and bad,*
> *happy or sad, true friends will be with you always,*
> *and no matter how often you hear it, diamonds are*
> *not a girl's best friend.*

Find your spirituality, find the desire to understand the
universe and your place in it, take time to notice the earth
and all of its beauty.

Take opportunities to get out and see the world, meet new people, get out of your comfort zone. Open your heart and mind to the tremendous world around you.

A firm handshake and good eye contact leave a lasting impression, yes, even from a woman. It not only represents self-confidence and ambition but also shows respect for the person you are dealing with. It's a sign that you are friendly, trustworthy, and honest. Be able to back it up!

Both men and women become your role models, so choose them carefully. A dad or other good male role model in your life becomes the standard against which you will assess all other men.

Do not allow yourself to become someone else's property. Be *you*, be true to who you are and don't ever let anyone else change that.

Accept yourself for who you are! You are one of a kind, and that's what makes you beautiful. Tall, short, small, blonde, brunette, redhead, white, black, we are all different, and that's what makes us uniquely beautiful.

Make your health a priority. Start now no matter your age; your health is your greatest asset. Be positive about your approach, and be aware of your physical, mental, social, emotional, and spiritual well-being. Healthy lifestyle choices, no matter when you start, will allow for continued wellness throughout your life. Diet, exercise, stress management, chiropractic, self-motivation, and meditation, as well as a number of other approaches, will have a huge impact on your quality of life, health, and happiness. Take the time to get a massage occasion-ally—take care of you.

Be a friend, be a protector. Fill your life with love and laughter; where there is love, there is life. Love is univer-sal and felt by all living things. So strong is the powerful feeling of love that it is said it makes the world go round.

Love is everywhere. It is God, and it lives inside of us. Love is why we are here. God has infinite amounts of Love for us and we are here to feel that Love and to show Love to one another. I believe that through our actions, every day, we have the chance to show Love and to change the world.

Chapter 13

Creating Your
Love Story

W hen all is said and done, I truly believe that love is all we have. I believe that this world, this complex and crazy place, is too much for us to handle on our own. It is bigger than we are, its meaning and purpose far exceed what we can imagine or understand. I believe we need to know that love, pure and true, is the foundation of this world and the reason for everything.

I believe that God is Love and Love is God. People are brought into our lives by divine intervention. For some of us this happens young, some later in life, for some, not until the second or third time around. For some it is "marriage" between a man and a woman, and for some it is through domestic partnership.

Do you ever stop to think that in this crazy push to become women of strength we might miss the opportunities that so many long for? While you're creating your love story, think about the things that you won't find in your life's organizer book. Think about the snuggling, the kissing, the sharing of stories, and the sharing of your thoughts, dreams, and desires. Look for the person who is standing beside you on your path. Reflect on your path to date and look at all there is still to travel. When choosing a partner in life, do all of the parts of 1 Corinthians apply?

> *Love is patient, love is kind. It does not envy, it does not boast, it is not proud. It does not dishonor others, it is not self-seeking, it is not easily angered, and it*

keeps no record of wrongs. Love does not delight in evil but rejoices with the truth. It always protects, always trusts, always hopes, and always perseveres.

If not, is this the life partner you wish to travel down the path with? I have seen the power of Love and what it does. I have felt it firsthand; I wish for you the same.

Personal Happiness Challenge: What is your love story?

Chapter 14

The 10-Step System to Personal Happiness

*O*ver the years, many women have approached me with questions about "personal happiness." At first, they might not call it that, but upon talking with each one, the conversation inevitably reveals two striking truths about their plight: First, many of these women are striving to reach their peak potential and are actively searching for solutions to many of the challenges and issues raised in this book. Second, in many cases the number-one obstacle they face is that they simply don't know where to start.

In this chapter, I share my 10-Step System to Personal Happiness with you. Starting with the end in mind, let me address why I call it Personal Happiness. Simply put, we who deal with the daily forces of balancing home life and a career create success when we craft and implement a custom-built plan that achieves personal happiness in our lives.

And now, on to the beginning: Where do you start?

First and foremost, *I want to challenge you!* To do that, let me say a brief word about goals: one of my mentors once told me that goals are merely the sequential actions we take to implement our *vision.*

Using that as our guidance, please take about thirty minutes to think about this powerful statement. When you're done, on a blank sheet of paper, I want you to write your vision *in the present tense,* and list five goals you believe you must achieve this coming year to fully implement that vision.

At this point, assuming you've completed the homework listed above, you are ready to bring my 10-Step System to Personal Happiness into your life. I would suggest that you review the list of steps below, and use a journal to capture any thoughts that come to mind as you study each item on the list.

Next, revisit those chapters in this book that tugged most strongly at your heart and mind. Ask yourself why those chapters struck such an emotional chord in you. View your answer to that question through the lens of the 10 steps below.

Finally, come back to this chapter, and create a 90-day action plan: for each of the 10 steps listed below, identify three actions you will take (and the date by when you will accomplish each action) to move yourself closer to your goals.

The 10-Step System to Personal Happiness

1. Love what you do, find your calling within your job, age doesn't matter, start today. Do your job with honesty, integrity, and discipline. The boss will notice, and if you're the boss, *you* will notice.

2. Give credit where credit is due, be grateful, and express your gratitude to whoever has helped you climb the ladder and to those who have been behind you pushing.

3. Educate yourself, reach out, read, learn, grow, and get better.

4. Stewardship: teach your children and those who look up to you how to do things correctly.

5. Write things down; make lists—not just for you but as a guide for those around you. Remember also to write notes of encouragement—and give them away.

6. Understand the difference between want and need—in your relationship, your purpose, and your financial life. Focus on the "needs," and, as you create success, reward yourself with a "want."

7. Take immediate steps to remedy or better all situations; don't wait for someone else to do it for you.

8. Choose your friends wisely—show me your friends and I'll show you your future. You'll know you're on the right path when you're consistently inspired and challenged to improve your results by the friends who surround you.

9. Separate the battles from the wars: be strategic as you decide where to place your energy.

10. Take the time to create your love story (see chapter 13), and read this chapter every 90 days to achieve your quest to personal happiness.

Resources

Your journey along the path towards personal happiness would never be complete without a list of key resources that could help you along the way. I've selected a range of resources that can help improve your financial acumen; your mind-set and self-image; and your ability to access the spiritual foundation found within each of us. Simply follow the Internet link for each resource listed below to acquire more information.

The Purpose Driven Life: What on Earth Am I Here For?
(Rick Warren)

Have you ever wondered why you are on this planet and what your "purpose" in life is? Unfortunately, many people allow many years in their life slip by before they begin exploring answers to these questions. A philosophy for Christian living in the 21st century, this book allows us to understand how God's plan affects each of our lives.

Website: http://purposedriven.com/books/pdlbook/#purpose

Simple Happiness (Jim Ryan)

Learn how to relax and be in the moment no matter how stressful each day is. As our attention gets drawn in so many different directions, it is important to learn how to bring ourselves back to a more focused and productive daily life.

Website: http://jimryantalks.com/

Biblica — Helping people worldwide to read the Bible

There are approximately 6,500 spoken languages and dialects worldwide; and approximately 4,000 languages for which Scripture has not yet been translated. Biblica reaches approximately 29 million people per year through printed and audio/visual Scripture resources.

Website: http://www.biblica.com/

Entrepreneur Success Stories, Volumes 1, 2, and 3

Best-selling authors Loral Langemeier and John C. Robinson help you to: (1) start your business by recognizing and acting on the entrepreneurial opportunities before you (volume 1); (2) generate income through effective marketing and sales strategies (volume 2); and implement the core principles of entrepreneurial growth and acceleration (volume 3).

Website: http://www.entrepreneur-success-stories.com/

Achieving Personal Happiness in Your Community
(Wendy Campbell)

If your clients or the members of your non-profit group or corporation are having difficulty in solving the work-life balance equation you will be glad to know that I am available to speak to your audience. Please see the web link below for all the details and the services I am able to provide to your group.

Website: http://mypersonalhappiness.com/speaker/

God's Cowboy Corner (Melinda Clements)

Using her writing as an avenue to witness and bring others to Christ, Melinda has formed and established her own ministry. It is called Perceptions Ministry and her God's Cowboy Corner branches off from there. Using her writing, her music, and her gift of counseling and insight she sends out daily devotionals online or through the mail in a monthly newsletter.

Website: http://www.melinda.clements.net/

Go For It! (John J. Tassone)

This is a practical guide to success which anyone can use. No matter what career you've chosen or are considering, John Tassone can help you hone your people skills, think positively, set long-range goals, and believe in your ability to achieve them.

Website: http://www.johntassone.com/

50 Women Every Christian Should Know
(Michelle DeRusha)

The world's history is rich with the stories of women who have applied faith and courage to step boldly forward and leave their indelible mark on those around them and on the kingdom of God. Michelle DeRusha tells their stories by focusing on fifty incredible heroines of the faith.

Website: http://michellederusha.com/50women/

About the Author

*W*endy Campbell is a small-town girl who lived her dream of becoming a wife, mother, and entrepreneur. Raised in a Colorado ranching community, she overcame many challenges and fulfilled her dreams with the support of excellent role models, her faith in God, and the love of a good man and two amazing children. Today, as a successful financial planner, she helps her clients build their legacy as they work toward a tax-free, reliable retirement.